a guide to

CORNWALL

by

WEEKEND JOURNALS

WORDS
Milly Kenny-Ryder

DESIGN
Simon Lovell

PHOTOGRAPHY
Gabriel Kenny-Ryder

weekendjournals.co.uk

CONTENTS

Our chosen places take you on a journey travelling around the Cornish coast.

PREFACE

There's something special about Cornwall. Perhaps it's the light, the blissful isolation, the evidence of a mysterious past or just the dramatic coastline. We have spent time exploring this enchanted county, meeting lots of the locals and becoming attuned to their slower pace of life. The shops have eccentric opening times based around the tides and the surf, and the restaurant kitchens close when the daily catch has all gone - it feels refreshing and healthy to live this way.

There are many celebrated places to visit time and time again in Cornwall, and I know frequent visitors often have a favourite haunt or ritual - a beach or an ice-cream shop they eagerly return to every trip. For us, it is the magical cloutie tree at Madron Wishing Well or enjoying a pasty from Philps after a bracing dip in the sea.

Although much of Cornwall's appeal is nostalgic, there are innovators who are bringing modern, stylish but sympathetic ideas to the Cornish scene: boutique hotels for hip travellers, gastronomic eateries for keen foodies and contemporary galleries and gardens to satisfy discerning aesthetes. Hopefully you will be encouraged to venture further afield to the exciting and special venues we have discovered, sometimes in the most unlikely corners.

There is so much more to experience in Cornwall than initially meets the eye, and I hope this book will inspire you to see and do more while visiting.

Milly Kenny-Ryder

St Ives
Penzance
Porthlev
Porthcurno
Isles of Scilly

Bude
Launceston
Port Isaac
Polzeath
Padstow
Bodmin
Newquay
Looe
St Austell
St Agnes
Truro
Falmouth
St Mawes
elston

TEMPLE

—

Restaurant & Shop

10 Granville Terrace, Bude, EX23 8JZ
templecornwall.com

Temple is a welcome addition to the North Cornwall town of Bude. This colourful eatery and shop opened in late 2017, a calming place to sit and relax while enjoying good food and organic wines.

Run by a team of four creatives, this innovative venue is a celebration of fashion and culture. The small boutique stocks a range of carefully curated lifestyle and clothing brands, such as Honest Skincare and Saturdays NYC.

The all-day food at Temple features bold flavours and fresh, wholesome ingredients, from brunch through to intimate dinner feasts. Coffee is made with Allpress beans and vibrant juices provide a health kick. In the evenings they introduce a sharing based ethos and regularly invite guest chefs to take part in their 'Temple Take-Over' residencies.

CEREAL

COOMBESHEAD FARM

—

Guesthouse & Restaurant

Lewannick, Launceston, PL15 7QQ
01566 782 009
coombesheadfarm.co.uk

Just five minutes' drive from the Devon-Cornwall border, Coombeshead Farm has everything you need for a weekend break. Founded by Pitt Cue Co-owner Tom Adams and Michelin-starred chef April Bloomfield, it is a foodie destination with beautiful bedrooms as a bonus. Set amongst sixty-six acres of meadows and woodland, this restaurant, guesthouse, working farm and bakery has a peaceful atmosphere that encourages you to feel at home.

The Georgian farmhouse has been designed by Ali Childs, of Studio Alexandra, who has thoughtfully juxtaposed rustic and retro countryside memorabilia with modern features and luxurious amenities.

Dinner is a highlight, cooked by Head Chef Tim Spedding and served in the renovated barn restaurant. The menu features produce from the farm used in an innovative way, naturally emphasising the essence of the area. Dinner and Sunday lunch are available to non-residents as well as staying guests.

The onsite bakery uses British stone ground flour to bake sourdough loaves and offers regular bread making workshops.

ST TUDY INN

—

Restaurant & Rooms

St Tudy, Bodmin, PL30 3NN
01208 850 656
sttudyinn.com

Emily Scott is an ambitious and optimistic chef, who took over this inn determined to offer locals and visitors great food and comfortable rooms in a delightful setting. The charming Cornish pub is situated in St Tudy, a quaint village in North Cornwall. After extensive redecoration, the pub feels cosy and welcoming with Nicole Heidaripour prints on the walls and vintage worn furniture.

All Emily's cheffing experience is put to good use in the kitchen, where seasonality and local produce reign. The menu is full of comforting classics with a twist; fish and chips for example is upgraded to the irresistibly tasty Monkfish tails in rosemary focaccia crumb with fries and citrus mayonnaise. The drinks list features a bespoke brew, The St Tudy Ale, made in collaboration with Padstow Brewing Co, and a one-off Malbec blend from the Civrac winery in Bordeaux.

Those who wish to extend their visit can stay in one of the simple, cosy bedrooms.

St Tudy Inn

RESTAURANT NATHAN OUTLAW

—

Restaurant

6 New Road, Port Isaac, PL29 3SB
01208 880 896
nathan-outlaw.com

A veritable prodigy of the kitchen, Nathan Outlaw worked under Gary Rhodes and Rick Stein before establishing his own reputation, opening the first two-Michelin-star fish restaurant in the UK. It is a clean, stylish dining room in Port Isaac with sharp service and immaculate seafood dishes.

Outlaw's food is blissfully minimalist, he aims 'to take ingredients away from the plate rather than add' which allows the Cornish produce, always cooked to perfection, to shine. The set menu features delights such as Gurnard with Porthilly Sauce, one of Outlaw's most elegant and brilliant recipes.

If you can't secure a table at the fine dining eatery, head to Port Isaac's charming harbour, where Nathan has opened his more relaxed Fish Kitchen, also to Michelin acclaim.

SURFSIDE

—

Restaurant & Bar

On the Beach, Polzeath, PL27 6TB
01208 862 931
surfsidepolzeath.com

Surfside is an exciting venture from London-based mixologist Tristan Stephenson, author of The Curious Bartender and co-founder of Purl and The Whistling Shop bars in London. Surfside has become a local hit, serving fresh food and cocktails at the water's edge in Polzeath. Located on a corner of the beach, the restaurant is only accessible via the sand, which adds to the experience.

Although the venue appears casual from the exterior, inside the offerings are for serious foodies with surf and turf platters and inventive cocktails. Thanks to the isolated location, Surfside feels intimate and exclusive with panoramic sea views adding something special to the meal.

Behind the main restaurant, a secret outdoor rum bar features live music in the summer months.

A Surfside FIELD-GUIDE
ILLUSTRATING A PERFECT DISECTION OF
HOMARUS GAMMARUS
CLAWS
KNUCKLES
LEGS & HEAD
TAIL
TAIL FANS

RIMINI, ITALY
MONDAY 9TH JUNE 2014

PADSTOW BREWING CO.

—

Shop & Tasting Room

6 Broad Street, Padstow, PL28 8BS
01841 533 110
padstowbrewing.co.uk

Padstow Brewing Co. is an independent microbrewery that produces a boutique range of artisan beers and ciders. Husband and wife team, Caron and Des Archer, began brewing in early 2013, testing out different equipment and recipes in an old surf-shower.

After establishing a successful method and recipes, Padstow Brewing Co. became a professional enterprise and proceeded to win numerous awards. The company has since expanded and now supplies some of the best foodie venues in Cornwall.

Their shop and tasting room in the centre of Padstow offers visitors a chance to taste the whole range, or buy gifts to take home.

Craft beer enthusiasts can also visit their brewery on the outskirts of town for an immersive brewing experience to fully understand the unique process.

PADSTOW
BREWING
CO.

PADSTOW
BREWING
CO.
A PINT OF PADSTOW
PADSTOW
BREWING
CO.
TASTING ROOM + GIFTS
PADSTOW
TASTING
ROOMS

APPLETON'S BAR AND RESTAURANT

—

Restaurant

Trevibban Mill, Dark Lane, near Padstow, PL27 7SE
01841 541 355
appletonsatthevineyard.com

Situated on the slopes of the Issey brook near Padstow, Appleton's has found its home above the successful Trevibban Mill winery. Ex-Fifteen head chef Andy Appleton heads up the kitchen and his partner Lyndsey manages the front of house.

The menu focuses on fine and flavoursome Italian dishes inspired by Andy's travels round Italy and his extensive experience working for Jamie Oliver. Choose from a beautiful piece of sustainable fish, or a bowl of comforting homemade pasta. The dishes provide the ideal accompaniment to a glass of Trevibban Mill wine, but there is also a range of Mediterranean drinks available.

Downstairs, Trevibban Mill produce award-winning Cornish wines. Tours and tastings at the winery can be arranged to sample the different wine and cider varieties.

THE SCARLET

—

Hotel

Tredragon Road, Mawgan Porth, Newquay, TR8 4DQ
01637 861 800
scarlethotel.co.uk

Perched on the rugged cliff tops overlooking Mawgan Porth, The Scarlet is the ultimate eco retreat. A rare, adults-only establishment in Cornwall, The Scarlet is an instantly calming place in which to spend time. It features fresh contemporary bedrooms, many of which boast private garden terraces or balconies, and an exemplary restaurant with seasonal dishes overseen by Head Chef Mike Francis.

The hotel proudly allows dogs in some rooms for a small fee per night, or if you fancy a bit of exercise on the beach, you can borrow the hotel dog, the ideal walking companion.

Downstairs, the destination spa offers Ayurvedic treatments to nourish body and soul and a soothing Relaxing Room with hanging cocoon pods for post-treatment sleeps. Rest in the outdoor sauna or soak in the cliff top hot tub which offers dramatic views across the Atlantic.

PAVILION

—

Café & Bakery

37 Fore Street, Newquay, TR7 1HD
pavilionbakery.com

A rare export from London, Pavilion opened shop on Fore Street in Newquay in 2017. This hipster café and bakery is much like its original stores in East London, stacked high with its celebrated sourdough bread and full of other appetising baked goods.

The Pavilion story began in Sri Lanka, where founder Rob fell in love with the country's culture, food and community. He returned home with a mission, and set up his first café in Victoria Park in London serving up signature Sri Lankan breakfasts and great speciality coffee and tea.

Pavilion opened several successful bakeries in London before making themselves at home in Newquay. Here you can find flaky pastries, seasonal Sri Lankan dishes and freshly baked sourdough bread, either to have in or to takeaway and enjoy on the beach.

PAVILION
PAVILION
BAKERY
FRESH BREAD,
PASTRIES &
COFFEE DAILY
BREAD.COFFEE.GOODS.
WWW.PAVILIONBAKERY.COM

WATERGATE BAY HOTEL

—

Hotel

On The Beach, Watergate Bay, Newquay, TR8 4AA
01637 860 543
watergatebay.co.uk

Watergate Bay Hotel, in North Cornwall, is set on one of the area's most spectacular beaches. With two miles of golden sand and an impressive swell from the Atlantic, it is a popular destination for surfers. Dolphins are also often spotted jumping through the azure sea. The hotel has light and laid-back double rooms, family suites and bunkrooms to choose from, making it suitable for both romantic getaways and family holidays. The decor is fresh and modern with splashes of colour and seaside artwork that reminds guests of their coastal location.

Downstairs, the stylish Swim Club offers an indoor infinity pool and private rooms for luxurious spa treatments. Food options are plentiful with four venues onsite including Zacry's for evening meals, casual seaside dining at The Beach Hut, and Italian cuisine at Jamie Oliver's Fifteen Cornwall. The Living Space is a calming place to sit with a glass of wine or a cocktail while watching the waves lap on the shore.

OPEN

—

Shop

Wheal Kitty Workshops, St Agnes, TR5 0RD
01872 553 918
open.surf

Open is a modern and satisfyingly minimalist surf shop located in the Wheal Kitty Workshops on the outskirts of St Agnes. Neighbouring a host of other creative businesses, this contemporary store enthusiastically serves local and visiting surfers.

The calm, cool space exhibits a range of handcrafted boards, in different styles and colours. Surf fans can come in and have a board made to their exact requirements and personalised to their wishes. Keen to involve the surfing community, the team offer 'Shaping' workshops, where you learn the basics of making a surfboard. Guest shapers also regularly visit the shop to make limited runs of exclusive boards.

Open is also a place to relax. There is a stylish seating area to sit with a cup of coffee and a piece of cake.

CANTEEN

—

Café & Events

9 Wheal Kitty Workshops, St Agnes, TR5 0RD
canteencornwall.com

Canteen is all about food with a cause. It is owned by husband and wife team, Ben and Sam Quinn, who gained a reputation with their inspiring catering company, Woodfired Canteen, which offers inventive and delicious cuisine for some of Cornwall's most exciting events.

Later they opened Canteen, in St Agnes, for the people of Cornwall to come together and eat wholesome food for a good price. Ben and Sam are passionate about giving back to the community and promoting the area in a healthy and sustainable way. They believe that their food outlet is about much more than just good food, hoping to offer people a great, positive atmosphere, good conversation and a place to meet with like-minded individuals.

Canteen is open each day for breakfast and lunch, and the menu changes regularly, with very reasonably priced vegetarian and meat options. There are also freshly baked cakes and Origin coffee for mid-morning or afternoon snacking.

CANTEEN
Breakfast
Coffee
Lunch
Cake

DOR & TAN

—

Pottery

The Studio at Glentworth, Carthew Terrace, St Ives, TR26 1EB
01736 799 318
dorandtan.com

The tradition of ceramics is intrinsically linked to St Ives and the Cornish coast. Dor & Tan is a ceramic design studio on the outskirts of St Ives, and the small team design, develop and create tableware for all occasions.

The team is led by head ceramicist Sharron who, along with Peter, Matthew and Viola, runs the small but efficient studio. Each handmade piece is created with love and care, with the intention of making something lasting to cherish but to enjoy using everyday. As well as developing their own range for shops across the country, the team design bespoke pieces for restaurants and coffee shops.

Dor & Tan is a rare example of modern but timeless pottery, which can be used regularly but appreciated for its beauty and design.

The working studio is open by appointment only but gives fans a special opportunity to pick and choose from the entire collection.

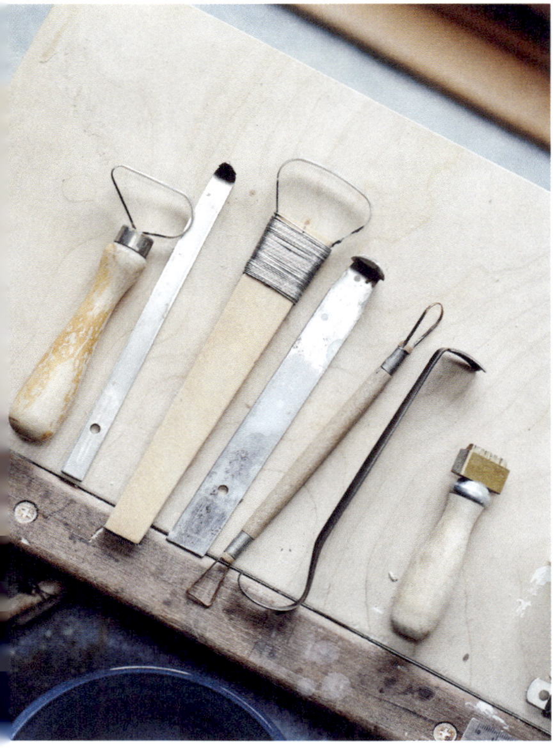

18
sun
feb

TATE ST IVES

—

Gallery

Porthmeor Beach, St Ives, TR26 1TG
01736 796 226
tate.org.uk

Tate St Ives reopened in Autumn 2017 after an extensive and dramatic refurbishment and expansion.

The famous art gallery is perched on the edge of Porthmeor Beach. Coastal daylight floods into the museum through the large windows and rooflights, illuminating the works and adding a magical glow to the rooms. With the renovation, the gallery space has doubled in size allowing much more art to be on display.

The gallery's permanent collection holds important works by modern British artists with a link to this area of Cornwall. You will find significant works by Barbara Hepworth, Peter Lanyon and Sandra Blow, amongst others.

On the top floor, Tate St Ives' café has the best panoramic views in town.

TREVOSE HARBOUR HOUSE

—

Hotel

22 The Warren, St Ives, TR26 2EA
01736 793 267
trevosehouse.co.uk

St Ives is the most popular town to visit in Cornwall, with a beautiful coastline and many cultural highlights. Located in the centre of town, Trevose Harbour House was reopened by Angela and Olivier Noverraz in 2013 after a full restoration. The six stylish bedrooms feel fresh and suit the seaside surroundings.

In the summer months, a suntrap terrace is a lovely place to relax, and in winter the cosy living room has an open fireplace and an honesty bar. Angela and Olivier take pride in the breakfast they provide: a feast of organic continental delights and an array of nourishing hot dishes.

For the best views of the harbour, book the rooftop suite, a glorious bedroom and bathroom decorated with accents of mid-century design while providing every luxury you could need.

ALBA

—

Restaurant & Bar

Old Lifeboat House, Wharf Road, St Ives, TR26 1LF
01736 797 222
alba-stives.co.uk

Upmarket and sophisticated, Alba is the ideal choice if you are looking for a special dinner in St Ives.

Owner and chef Grant Nethercott pursued his long-term dream to open a restaurant, setting up Alba in St Ives' former lifeboat house in 2002. Over the last decade the eatery has evolved, catering to changing food trends. The menu, although influenced by classical French dining, is mainly led by the fine British produce of the area and in particular line-caught fish. The dishes are big on flavour and artistically plated, making the food at Alba a joy to see and taste.

Alba's dining room has beautiful views overlooking the beach and Grant exhibits his impressive private art collection on the walls, reminding guests of St Ives' artistic tradition.

BARBARA HEPWORTH MUSEUM AND SCULPTURE GARDEN

—

Museum

Barnoon Hill, St Ives, TR26 1AD
01736 796 226
tate.org.uk

Nestled among tropical shrubs and exotic flowers stand the solemn sculptures of Barbara Hepworth, Cornwall's leading lady.

The Trewyn Studios appear as if untouched since Hepworth ended her days here in 1975 and the workshop and intimate garden have a quiet, peaceful atmosphere. Sheltered from the fierce coastal winds, it is a fertile oasis, especially in spring when the blossom is out. The garden is particularly enchanting early in the morning before all the tourists arrive.

St Ives has a long history as a home for major artists, potters and sculptors, but Barbara Hepworth was undoubtedly the most prolific and potent.

SANDS & SAMPHIRE STUDIOS

—

Holiday Apartments

Beach Court, Porthgwidden, St Ives, TR26 1PL
01736 317 740
stives-studios.co.uk

Quietly tucked away on St Ives' Island are the stylish Sands and Samphire studios. These beautifully designed apartments are owned and run by Angela and Olivier Noverraz, of Trevose Harbour House.

Spacious yet cosy, the studios each provide a luxurious and private retreat for couples wishing to escape the busy central hub of this popular coastal town. Themed by colour, the rooms are decorated with carefully chosen vintage furniture and artistic details.

Samphire Studio is found on the ground floor with a vibrant green decor inspired by its exotic garden. Upstairs, Sands Studio offers particularly magnificent views of the sea and golden beaches, and the unique furniture echoes the yellow hues. The apartments have all the necessary amenities to ensure you truly find a home away from home.

food

PLUMBLINE

—

Shop

2 Barnoon Hill, St Ives, TR26 1AD
07703 797 060
plumblinestives.co.uk

Plumbline is a discreet design shop well worth seeking out. The small space is perfectly curated - a pristine gallery for stylish shoppers wishing to discover something exceptional.

Deborah, the imaginative owner, handpicks items from a variety of talented artists from all over the country. Plumbline's stock is a stark contrast to the seaside memorabilia that fills the more touristy shops. Jochen Holz, the East London glassblower has a range of his striking work here, as well as elegant ceramics by Sam Hall.

Behind the shop there is a small, good-looking flat for visitors to rent; a design haven for the aesthetically inclined traveller.

PORT OF CALL

—

Shop

9 Market Place, St Ives, TR26 1RZ
01736 796 211
academyandco.com

Port of Call is the third retail space from Kate and James Deseta, a brother and sister team who are bringing clean aesthetics and a love of design to St Ives.

The carefully displayed homeware items and magazines are sure to induce domestic envy. The shop stocks niche brands - there is organic skincare by Grown Alchemist from Australia, Ondine Ash's ethically-produced patterned cushions and beautiful ceramics from St Ives' own Dor & Tan. Alongside the lifestyle items, there is a selection of pretty house plants and accessories, and you can also stock up on speciality journals and inspiring travel books.

Nearby, their clothing store, Academy & Co stocks diverse designers like Norse Projects and Ally Capellino, while a third shop, Number 8 focuses on streetwear and trainers.

UPRISING
FIFTY FASHION DESIGNERS ONE CITY
PHAIDON
Nautical Chic
GIFT WRAP SHEETS
WITH GIFT TAGS & TWINE
D-CLIPS
THE SPORTSMAN
The Silver Spoon Kitchen
Recipes from an Italian
THE PALESTINIAN TABLE
Reem Kassis

LEACH POTTERY

—

Museum

Higher Stennack, St Ives, TR26 2HE
01736 799 703
leachpottery.com

St Ives is a notably artistic area of Britain with a long list of influential painters and potters making their home here. Founded in 1920 by Bernard Leach and Shoji Hamada as a place for potters to train and learn their trade, Leach Pottery is one of the most famous ceramic institutions in the UK.

Today, the pottery continues to operate as a working studio with the museum and gallery offering an insight into its history. The exhibition space presents the work of international and local potters, with occasional residencies from celebrated artists from around the world.

There is also a shop onsite where you can purchase a special piece from the Leach Standard Ware range.

THE MINACK THEATRE

—

Theatre

Porthcurno, TR19 6JU
01736 810 181
minack.com

Concealed within the scenic cliffs of Porthcurno is the enchanting Minack Theatre. The project was first imagined and built by Rowena Cade, who lived in Minack House nearby. From 1931, Rowena and her gardener tirelessly moved boulders to create a space for actors to perform, and tiered steps to accommodate spectators. The first production, a version of The Tempest, was performed in this curious venue in 1932 and the theatre is still very much in use during the warmer months.

With the turquoise waters lapping at Porthcurno Beach in the background, it is a dramatic and magical setting in which to witness any play. You can also visit during the day, when there is no performance, to view the site and learn about the theatre's history.

THE TOLCARNE INN

—

Pub & Restaurant

Newlyn, Penzance, TR18 5PR
01736 363 074
tolcarneinn.co.uk

Chef Ben Tunnicliffe has given his time and expertise to the Cornwall food scene for almost two decades. After being awarded one of the first Michelin stars in the county, Ben has returned to a simpler style of cooking, with less fuss and more focus on flavour.

This characterful pub is a favourite with all Penzance dwellers; locals treasure it and tourists flock to it for a hearty Sunday lunch. The inn has been around since 1717, and the low-beamed ceilings and wood-burning fire ensure it is always cosy and welcoming.

Ideally located next door to the famous Newlyn Fish Market, Ben relishes the opportunity to cook the freshest local seafood. The regularly changing menu is written each morning on a blackboard and reflects the day's catch and the flavours of the season. Ben is instinctive in the kitchen, so that even the simplest plates of food sparkle here.

TOLCARNE INN

SEA FISH
SALTVANDSFISK
SEEFISCHE
seafood delicatessen

ARTIST RESIDENCE

—

Hotel

20 Chapel Street, Penzance, TR18 4AW
01736 365 664
artistresidence.co.uk

Chapel Street seems a fitting home for the Cornish branch of Artist Residence. This boutique property opened in 2010 as the second hotel in a rapidly growing group.

The Artist Residence hotels are full of flair and personality thanks to the young and entrepreneurial couple behind the business. Justin and Charlie Salisbury originally asked local artists to design and paint the bedrooms at this quaint Penzance hotel in exchange for board, and some of these artistic rooms still remain today.

The hotel now has 22 eclectically decorated bedrooms and a three-bedroom cottage for families or groups. The rooms bring the essence of Penzance indoors, with seaside-inspired artwork, antique furniture and a minibar stocked with Cornish treats. One of the most popular bedrooms is number 17, a small but beautiful room with plenty of natural light and an indulgent roll-top bathtub.

The resident restaurant, The Cornish Barn, serves hearty dishes and there is also a living room bar area for enjoying a drink by the fire.

REGENT BUILDINGS

La Vita

THE SHORE

Restaurant

13/14 Alverton Street, Penzance, TR18 2QP
01736 362 444
theshorerestaurant.uk

Bruce Rennie is one of the chefs leading the exciting, quickly evolving food scene in Penzance. After gaining experience at prestigious restaurants such as Michelin-starred Martin Wishart in Edinburgh, Bruce moved to Cornwall to head up the kitchen at the Gurnard's Head before opening his own eatery in September 2015.

The restaurant, which occupies the Old Buttery, is decorated in shades of blue with subtle seaside motifs. Although there are no sea views, Bruce more than compensates with the flavoursome and creative plates of food. His dishes showcase the fishermen's daily catch and champion ingredients that the area produces in abundance.

For a special occasion, the private dining room can be hired for a refined seafood tasting menu.

NO. 56

—

Shop

14 Chapel Street, Penzance, TR18 4AW
01736 366 293
no-56.com

Chapel Street in Penzance is a shopper's paradise with an assortment of unique design and retro outlets. On a sunny afternoon, it is a lovely lane to explore, stopping at each shop to rummage through the vintage trinkets or peruse the desirable objects and garments.

After a career in mens and womenswear design, Carole Elsworth set up No. 56 where she uses her experience to put together a personal collection based on natural materials and simple designs.

The shop has a fine assortment of stationery and homeware, displayed in a fresh minimalist setting. Pick up a bottle of J Herbin violet-scented ink, a couple of beeswax candles or a minimalist ceramic piece by local potter, Rebecca Proctor. Carole is constantly expanding the range to include her own label 'Handworked' alongside her latest favourite finds, from Cornwall and further afield.

Nº56

CHAPEL HOUSE

—

Hotel

Chapel Street, Penzance, TR18 4AQ
01736 362 024
chapelhousepz.co.uk

This beautiful, restored townhouse is on the corner of Chapel Street, one of Penzance's most picturesque roads. With views overlooking the sea and St Michael's Mount, it is in an enviable position. Owner Susan Stuart saw an opportunity to renovate and refresh this grand historic building, previously the home of the Penzance Arts Club, offering Penzance visitors a serene and luxurious place to stay.

The boutique hotel has six double bedrooms to choose from and each is thoughtfully designed with a mix of antique pieces and modern amenities. Reclaimed 1930s office lamps frame the bespoke beds, and a mini iPad in each room allows you to video call for room service should you need it. Room 2 is particularly beautiful with an Ashton & Bentley bathtub and lots of natural light. Wherever possible, Susan supports local makers and suppliers; toiletries are sourced from Penzance beauty brand, Pure Nuff Stuff, and the artwork on the walls is loaned from Newlyn School of Art.

Susan's delicious breakfasts and dinners are enjoyed in the communal dining room, where you can also find wellies for muddy walks and blankets to borrow on chillier days.

JUBILEE POOL

—

Lido & Café

Battery Road, Penzance, TR18 4FF
01736 369 224
jubileepool.co.uk

Recently restored to its former glory, Jubilee Pool is once again the pride of Penzance. It was originally designed by Captain F. Latham in the early 1930s and the unique Art Deco shape is said to complement the behaviour of the surrounding waves. Where possible, original details have been kept, notably the welcoming 'Bathing Pool' sign and the cubist influenced changing rooms.

Surprisingly, Jubilee is one of the only remaining saltwater tidal pools left in Europe. The main pool is suitable for all swimmers, while a smaller pool accommodates young children.

A relaxed café at the poolside is a welcome addition for athletic visitors needing sustenance or a refreshing drink. The lido is a glorious spot for summer swims or family picnics, and the brilliant blue pools are a beautiful addition to the Penzance coast.

DEEP
END

TREMENHEERE SCULPTURE GARDENS

—

Gallery & Gardens

near Gulval, Penzance, TR20 8YL
01736 448 089
tremenheere.co.uk

This vast and verdant garden in Penzance is definitely not just for art enthusiasts; the route through the epic plants and trees will transport you from the moment you step inside. A short drive from the town, Tremenheere is a dramatic setting for impressive sculptural works both permanent and temporary. The unique positioning and climate allow exotic plants and flowers to flourish, creating a tropical world. From the top of the hill there are magical vistas of St Michael's Mount and the coastline.

Renowned artists such as Richard Long, Peter Randall-Page and Tim Shaw have interacted with the landscape to create specific works that complement the setting, but James Turrell's Skyspace (Tewlwolow Kernow) is perhaps the most mesmerising work, an oval space showing the ever-changing sky. In wetter weather, the two-storey timber art gallery is a lovely indoor space, featuring some of the finest artists in West Cornwall.

After exploring the gardens, visit Tremenheere Kitchen for wholesome food and the shop, Artisan, for a small selection of thoughtful gifts.

ORIGIN COFFEE ROASTERS, HARBOUR HEAD

—

Coffee Shop

Harbour Head, Porthleven, TR13 9JY
origincoffee.co.uk

Established in 2004 by a group of enthusiasts, Origin specialise in sourcing and roasting exceptional coffee. The company was founded in Cornwall and their Roastery is available for tours, with prior booking.

In 2013, Origin opened a café at Harbour Head in Porthleven, supplying locals with high quality coffee and a cool, contemporary venue in which to drink it. On a quiet afternoon in this sleepy seaside town, Origin is the perfect place to enjoy the views with one of their speciality single origin coffees and a slice of artisan cake. The team has opened a second larger café in Penryn for Cornwall caffeine fans.

Due to its popularity, Origin has also set up shop in London, with cafés in Shoreditch, Hammersmith and an outpost in The British Library.

Please mind
the step

NEW YARD

—

Restaurant

Trelowarren, Mawgan, Helston, TR12 6AF
01326 221 595
newyardrestaurant.co.uk

Those who know about New Yard visit regularly, raving about the wholesome food and lovely laid-back atmosphere.

The restaurant is found in the historic old stableyard deep within Trelowarren Estate, close to the Lizard, which is the southernmost tip of Cornwall. The rugged natural gardens of Trelowarren are alluring and unspoilt, and it would be easy to get lost wandering around the picturesque grounds.

New Yard is spacious and welcoming with rustic tables and a roaring fire in the winter. The chefs hail from some of the county's finest restaurants, and whip up seasonal and fresh dishes with pride and enthusiasm. The food is unfussy and delicious, with a priority on local fish. In the summer months there is also a pizzeria for homemade, wood-fired pizzas.

THE SANDY DUCK

—

Bed & Breakfast

12 Pennance Road, Falmouth, TR11 4EA
01326 311 427
thesandyduck.co.uk

The Sandy Duck, just outside Falmouth, is a relaxing and calm place to stay. This stylish, boutique B&B has seven bedrooms and is decorated in pale shades with a Scandinavian aesthetic in mind. The contemporary design is interspersed with unique antique furniture and special family mementos and artwork.

Owner-manager Freyja previously spent time aboard luxury yachts cooking and crewing before arriving in Cornwall to open The Sandy Duck. She poured her time and care into transforming this Edwardian townhouse into a lovely minibreak retreat.

Many of the rooms offer sea views, while others feature indulgent freestanding bathtubs. Breakfast is served in the airy dining room downstairs where Freyja cooks up tempting delights.

TORO

—

Shop

Old Brewery Yard, High Street, Falmouth, TR11 2BY
toro-studio.com

Falmouth is a town of creatives and has spawned many inventive projects and businesses. Toro is found in the Old Brewery Yard, among a number of artistic boutiques - it is a small and lush botanical studio crowded with whimsical hanging plants and shelves of cacti. The plants look at home on the shop's attractive wood furniture, some of which is created by local designer, Heather Scott.

Toro owner, Tor Harrison, champions plants for indoor spaces and believes plants have the power to change the dynamics of a space, adding character while lifting the mood.

Pick a plant or choose from Toro's range of Bashō and Honest skincare and candles in suitably green flavours like Eucalyptus Leaf. To keep your succulents healthy ask Tor for advice on how to water and nurture them.

honest

ESPRESSINI

—

Café

39 Killigrew St, Falmouth, TR11 3PW
espressini.co.uk

There are more and more promising independent coffee shops in Cornwall; Espressini on Killigrew Street in Falmouth is one of the best. This characterful venue serves a bespoke selection of single-farm beans sourced and roasted by Yallah Coffee, selected specially for them from growers around the world. Inside, the café is cosy and familiar with mismatched antique furniture, and the chatter is accompanied by a thoughtful playlist.

The coffee is bold in flavour and served to your preference. Brunch is particularly popular with a menu of tempting and indulgent dishes displaying a wide range of influences from world cuisines.

Nearby, on Falmouth Harbour, is Dulce, the smaller sibling of Espressini which, as well as offering freshly brewed coffee, sells equipment to help you make the perfect cup at home.

FOLKLORE

—

Shop

Old Brewery Yard, High Street, Falmouth, TR11 2BY
folklorefalmouth.co.uk

Folklore is tucked away in Falmouth's Old Brewery Yard, a courtyard full of creative businesses. It is a serene and beautiful store stocking a carefully curated range of functional and aesthetic products from young local designers.

The shop is owned by Hannah Lawrence and presents her quirky ceramics alongside a variety of handcrafted objects, such as contemporary woodwork by Felix McCormack and delicate jewellery by Ellie Hughes. Sarah Johnson's hand-dyed indigo smocks are both unique and wearable, and inventive recycled bags are a boyish addition by Francli.

Despite its limited size, the shop has enough stock to keep visitors intrigued, especially if you are keen to hear the story behind each desirable item. The collection is constantly evolving as the makers are inspired by their Cornish surroundings to create new works.

Hannah also owns Cup Studio nearby, which is solely dedicated to pinch pottery.

STAR & GARTER

—

Pub & Rooms

52 High Street, Falmouth, TR11 2AF
01326 316 663
starandgarter.squarespace.com

Falmouth is usually the first city in Cornwall to catch on to food trends, with every cuisine readily available. Star & Garter is found at the top of the High Street with staggering views over the boats in the bay.

This historic maritime pub was recently taken over by Becca and Elliot Thompson, who have given the property a new lease of life with their vision and enthusiasm. Elliot looks after the stoves with his passionate team of chefs, while Becca manages the front of house. The menu showcases lesser-used cuts of meat and local fish, all sourced from nearby producers. They have become particularly well known for their spectacular Sunday roasts.

After stripping back and renovating the building, Becca and Elliot put in three luxurious bedrooms upstairs for guests who wish to stay at Star & Garter for a little longer.

BEACON COFFEE

—

Coffee Shop

28a High Street, Falmouth, TR11 2AD
beaconcoffee.co.uk

The speciality coffee movement is gathering momentum in Cornwall, and Falmouth is benefitting more than most.

Beacon Coffee was opened in early 2018 by a team of expert baristas who hail from longstanding coffee house Espressini. The modern, Scandi-inspired space is an inviting place to catch up with friends or to quietly work, while being fuelled by expertly sourced and poured coffee.

Owners Sam and Alex pride themselves on offering a menu of unique and unusual brews and pours, developing the latest trends and investigating alternative methods of making and drinking coffee. They use a constantly rotating selection of beans, including Old Spike and Colonna.

Opt for the 'one + one', a single-shot flat white with an extra shot of espresso on the side, allowing you to taste and appreciate the same coffee bean in two different ways.

"The best coffee maker I've ever owned."
"The best coffee maker I've ever owned."
V60 Dripper
V60 Dripper
OLD SPIKE
OLD SPIKE

BEACON COFFEE

POTAGER GARDEN

—

Café

High Cross, Constantine, Falmouth, TR11 5RF
01326 341 258
potagergarden.org

Nestled in the enchanting Constantine countryside, Potager Garden is a lovely place to spend time, indulging in a healthy vegetarian feast in the greenhouse or a refreshing drink in the sunshine outside. This daytime café was an abandoned plant nursery before it was transformed into a picturesque haven for eating and relaxing. The chefs, led by Daisy Hillier, use organic produce from the gardens to create vibrant and delicious recipes.

Six studios onsite are used by resident artists and frequent Open Studio days allow the public to view the work for free. The surrounding gardens are constantly evolving, with a wealth of beautiful flowers, so it is always a rewarding place to visit.

On occasion, Potager Garden also host evening meals, from lively banquets to fine dining feasts.

NANCARROW

—

Farm & Feasts

Zelah, near Truro, TR4 9DQ
01872 487 099
nancarrowfarm.co.uk

The feast nights at Nancarrow Farm have become renowned across West Cornwall; popular with locals and visitors, they sell out fast. Primarily a family-run farm, the scenic 100-acre grounds produce an abundance of high quality organic meats. For nine generations the farmers, their family and friends have eaten around the kitchen table enjoying hearty home-cooked dishes and home-brewed Barn Ale.

With a professional kitchen onsite, the team is now able to welcome guests to memorable events, private cookery workshops and exciting feast nights. Each month a new menu is designed around the farm's own produce; everything is cooked in a wood-fired oven with live music providing an atmospheric accompaniment.

There are also eight charming en-suite bedrooms and tipis in the orchard for guests to book, if staying over.

TREGOTHNAN

—

Gardens & Tea Room

The Woodyard, Tresillian, Truro, TR2 4AJ
01872 520 000
tregothnan.co.uk

Supplying some of Britain's most prestigious tearooms, Tregothnan is a prime example of a fine English brand. Home to the Boscawen family since 1334, this is where the first English tea in the UK was planted as recently as 1999. The extensive, manicured gardens are home to a variety of interesting exotic plants and a thriving Camellia sinensis tea crop. The heritage site and gardens are only accessible to guests if a guided tour is booked in advance.

After a bracing walk, afternoon tea can be provided in the café accompanied, of course by Tregothnan tea in a range of flavours. This luxurious Cornish tea can be found in celebrated hotels and tearooms across the country, including Fortnum & Mason and The Mandarin Oriental Hyde Park.

DRIFTWOOD

—

Hotel & Restaurant

Rosevine, Portscatho, St Mawes, TR2 5EW
01872 580 644
driftwoodhotel.co.uk

Driftwood, with its dramatic sea views and its own private beach, is set among acres of lush green gardens, just a short drive from St Mawes. The classic bedrooms are decorated in a fresh seaside style, with striped materials and beach themed features.

The hotel's Michelin-starred restaurant is reason alone to visit Driftwood. It is open just for adults and only in the evenings, when chef Chris Eden creates impeccable dishes showcasing the best local produce with innovation and flair. The menu changes regularly though a favourite, like the striking 'Thunder and Lightning Tart' with saffron jelly and ginger beer, is a firm fixture.

For lunch, order a filled picnic basket to enjoy after a walk on the beach. Hidden Hut is another dining option nearby, a secretive café with a wholesome menu.

HOTEL TRESANTON

—

Hotel

27 Lower Castle Rd, St Mawes, TR2 5DR
01326 270 055
tresanton.com

Celebrating its 20th year in 2018, Tresanton was the first design conscious hotel in Cornwall and is a favourite for many sojourning in the South West. It is located on the sea's edge, in the quaint fishing village of St Mawes, and guests can enjoy spectacular views from every room.

Owned and designed by the illustrious Olga Polizzi, the space evokes her personality and style in even the smallest details. Bedrooms feature an eclectic mix of vintage furniture and luxurious fabrics, whilst the modern bistro and terraces are relaxed places to spend time. In the warmer months, the Beach Club is a breezy oasis to enjoy casual cuisine and magnificent views.

Don't miss a trip out on the hotel's famed Pinuccia, an immaculately restored 1930s wooden sail boat. This classic yacht is beautiful enough on still waters, but on a windy day is a real Cornish coastal experience.

ISLES OF SCILLY

—

Islands

Those in the know about British travel, take an annual pilgrimage to the Isles of Scilly. Of the 1500 or so islands in the archipelago, only five are inhabited. After a short flight or boat journey from the mainland to St Mary's, the other islands are accessible by water taxi just ten minutes or less apart. The serene waters and warm climate provide an idyllic retreat for visitors and a safe, quiet lifestyle for the islanders.

Choose an island destination dependent on what you desire from a holiday, Tresco for luxurious bliss, Bryher for a rugged remote escape or St Agnes for an isolated artistic retreat. Accommodation varies from campsites to rented sea-view cottages, or for something extra special book in to Hell Bay Hotel. Local restaurants celebrate the produce from the surrounding ocean and communal feasting at The Crab Shack is not to be missed.

There are plenty of sea-based activities to enjoy, and on land the Tresco Abbey Garden is the most visited attraction. With hundreds of exotic plants, flowers and trees carefully selected from all over the world and immaculately nurtured, it is quite a spectacle, especially when the sun shines.

MIKE NELHAMS

—

CURATOR, TRESCO ABBEY GARDEN

Mike Nelhams began his Horticultural career at the Royal Horticultural Society Garden Wisley, in Surrey. Following this, he was awarded a year's scholarship to study in the Abbey Garden under the renowned plantsman and then Head Gardener Peter Clough. After completing his scholarship, Mike spent five years in Sussex before being offered the Head Gardener position at Tresco by Robert Dorrien-Smith, and he has been on the island ever since. Mike says his career and life has been totally defined by the Abbey Garden and its unique collections. His wife Isobel was born on Tresco and so were his two daughters, so it's where they all call home.

Can you tell us a bit about the history of Tresco Island and of Tresco Abbey Garden.

For me, the history of Tresco Island began when Augustus Smith took the lease of all the islands in 1834. He and his family shaped the islands to become what they are today, introducing school education, churches, housing, and the beginnings of the Tresco Abbey Garden. Through five family generations, the garden - with its ability to grow tender plants from tropical areas of the world such as South Africa, Australia, California, South America and the Canary Islands - has gone from strength to strength and is now considered as one-of-a-kind within the gardening world.

What do you like best about Tresco, and the Isles of Scilly in general?

Tresco is a very special place, within a special group of islands. On an English coastline you simply look out to sea. Here on Scilly, there is always an alternative view out to another island, and this view is ever changing due to the tide, light and weather conditions. It means every day is different. With our many white sandy beaches and clear blue seas, you couldn't wish to be anywhere else. Our climate here on Scilly is unique in the British Isles; it rarely gets too cold, never gets too hot and has just about the right amount of rainfall in which to sustain our special plant collections.

What does your role as Curator at Tresco Abbey Garden involve?

Managing a modern garden today is a very varied role. Two days are never the same, but typically I look after staff training, international plant health regulations, garden tours, plant procurement, student engagement and the perils of modern machinery.

Which plants, flowers and trees native to Cornwall particularly excite you?

Cornwall is probably considered to be the finest "Garden County" in the country. It has amassed many plants that were brought in by the great Victorian plant hunters that were employed by the garden owners of the time. So, although not 'native' to Cornwall, but very important and thought of as in-house, are the fine Cambellii Magnolia trees that can be seen at Caerhays Castle and the Rhododendron collections at Trewithen, Trellisick and Glendurgan. With its favoured climate, Cornish gardens have a wide diversity that is much admired by the rest of the country.

And which imported plants do you have here that are particularly interesting or unique to Tresco?

We have recently introduced the well-named "Cabbage Tree" from Robinson Crusoe Island. As far as we are aware, we are the only garden in Britain to grow this plant out of doors with no artificial protection. It has the most splendidly large glossy leaves that grow up to a metre long and has drooping yellow flowers. Probably the most important and spectacular group in the garden are the Proteaceae family - no one can fail to notice the impressive "King Protea" with its flowers up to twelve inches across.

So you must have visited gardens around the world, is there one that stands out?
One garden for me stands alone. It was started by a man called Sir Thomas Hanbury, in the small Italian village of La Mortola on the French-Italian border very near Monte Carlo. The reason it has such importance to me is that each year, usually in February, the whole Abbey Garden team travel out and stay with the Hanbury family. We always come back to Tresco reinvigorated with fresh ideas and new plants to add to our terraces.

What do you want people to feel while experiencing the gardens?
I think the great thing about the Abbey Garden is that even someone who'd consider themselves a non-gardener can find a sudden interest, simply by walking through our terraces and finding themselves being overshadowed by exotic Palm trees up to forty-foot-tall...If you were parachuted into the centre of the garden and asked which country you had landed into, I don't think many people would guess England.

As well as plants and trees, there are quite a few sculptures – tell us a bit about these.
Robert and Lucy Dorrien-Smith, who own Tresco Island, regard art as a very important feature – their private art collection is available to view across the island and within the garden. The standout pieces are David Wynne's Tresco Children and his Mother Earth figure, Gaia, along with the Agave Fountain and the Garden Archways by local sculptor Tom Leaper. Over the years, many artists and sculptors have visited to put their own interpretation on what they see, which in turn make a great addition and contrast to our plant collection.

Can you tell us about any important people that you've given a tour of the gardens too?
We have had many well known and important faces visit us over the years. I've given tours to members of the Royal family from The Queen Mother to, more recently, Prince William and Kate. We have also had visits from ex-Prime Minister John Major, actors Helen Mirren and Judi Dench, and photographer David Bailey, to name but a few. Of course, not forgetting the well-known TV gardener, Alan Titchmarsh, who has filmed with us on many occasions.

How have you seen Cornwall and the Isles of Scilly change in the time you've been here?
What I really like about the changes in both Cornwall and Scilly in the 35 years I have been here, is that they are all for the good. The quality and choice of accommodation has improved considerably - eco and boutique hotels have sprung up complementing the fabulous holiday experiences available here. And Cornwall has become a real "foodie" destination across the county. Also, environmental considerations such as cleaner beaches, the fight against plastic (led by groups such as Surfers Against Sewage), and better appreciation for wildlife, are all changes for the better.

What are your favourite things to do or places to go to in the Isles of Scilly and Cornwall?
I am a great fan of the Cornish landscape, particularly with the sea being such a strong influence. When in Cornwall, it is a real treat to take advantage of both the North and South coasts, as both are so very different. The rugged cliffs of the North coast around Rock and Polzeath combined with the golf courses of St Enodoc and Trevose make a jolly weekend for me, when time allows. The South Coast having a much softer atmosphere, with its wooded creeks and valleys, gives time to explore and visit some of the many hidden public and private gardens that inhabit the more sheltered coastline.

NATHAN OUTLAW

CHEF

Nathan Outlaw began cooking as a child with his chef father, before continuing into formal food training. After working extensively with Rick Stein and Paul Ripley in Cornwall, he fell in love with Cornish produce, especially the fish. In 2003 he opened his first solo venture, The Black Pig, for which he received a Michelin star, aged just 25. He went on to establish two restaurants in Port Isaac, Restaurant Nathan Outlaw (RNO), recognised as the only two star fish restaurant in the UK, and the more relaxed Outlaw's Fish Kitchen. He also has eateries in London and Dubai, and runs The Mariners Public House in Rock.

What's your story? Why Cornwall?
I grew up in Kent but came on holiday to Cornwall as a child every year. I first came to live and work here aged 19. I had been working in London as a young commis and in every restaurant I seemed to gravitate towards the fish station, and soon decided I wanted to concentrate on fish. Rick Stein was the fish god so I came down to Cornwall to work for him and fell in love with it. In Stein's restaurant I met my wife over the hot plate, a local girl who was working front of house. I spent two years working for Rick, which included a whole year just prepping seafood. Over my time there Stein had become huge and Padstow was no longer a sleepy fishing town.

I loved Cornwall but needed more experience so moved to Lords of the Manor Hotel in the Cotswolds and then the Vineyard at Stockcross, in both working for John Campbell, a very good Michelin-starred chef. Before long I came back to Cornwall and opened my first restaurant, the Black Pig in 2003. With just me in the kitchen, at only 25 years old, it was very hard work. I never knew much about Michelin stars... but after eight months the Black Pig was awarded one.

I then went on to open my fine dining restaurant and fish kitchen, both in Port Isaac. Everything in my restaurants is inspired by the sea and local produce.

You've also got your London restaurant... how do you cater differently there?
It is all fish at RNO but in London there are meat options (although the menu is still predominantly seafood). Also, in London, the fish is delivered from the sea six or seven hours later. We've got a very efficient transfer – the fish goes on to the train at Penzance, straight to Paddington where it is picked up by electric cars to take it to the restaurant. I know the fishermen, and I know exactly where it comes from so I'm confident that it's the best fish in London.

How have you seen Cornwall change in the time you've been here?
It's changed in a big way. Some Cornish people may not agree, but I think Rick had a massive effect on the county. He brought awareness that there are amazing ingredients and food here. When I first came, there wasn't the variety there is now. You can eat really well all over Cornwall, there's a great Asian restaurant in Newquay (called Kahuna) and a street food place in Truro which is fantastic – the reason they are so good is because the owners have travelled the world surfing and eating in all these different countries, so they know how to make authentic food. The pubs have improved a lot too – they've had to up their game because of everything else around them.

Cornwall has become a foodie destination,

and we've noticed that a large number of our customers visit as part of a foodie tour, trying different cuisines all around the county.

Are there any recent restaurants that you think are particularly exciting?
Appleton's Restaurant and Coombeshead Farm are the two most exciting recent openings in Cornwall. The Shore in Penzance is also great and Porthminster Café has a lovely location with amazing views.

You said your style is based on the sea… how do you define it?
Probably the one thing is… I'm always looking to take things away from a plate. When you're a young chef you're trying to show all your skills, but for me it's more about getting the best out of the ingredients. The guys we use for vegetables (a father and son) are not specialists in micro herbs or anything fancy, but they grow proper onions and carrots, which make a huge difference in the depth of flavour compared to a sack of regular onions. If you eat something that's been done properly you'll notice it, the simplest dishes can blow you away.

In France or Italy, you can go to a market and you buy better produce than they serve in a restaurant. There's no excuse for bad food. The tomatoes we get are from Rob Hocking at Buttervilla Growers near Looe, he doesn't produce as much as other growers because he prunes the vines; he goes for quality and the flavour is so incredible. When I started I said to Chris (former head chef at RNO) that I wanted to get to the point where I could just put a great piece of fish and sauce on a plate, he laughed and said you can't do that, but now we do…

Is there a fish that you think is underrated? Or you'd like to use more…
There's fish I'd like to use that I don't. I love octopus for example, but I can't get it from the sea here in Cornwall. We use it in the fish kitchen and the pub, but RNO only uses fish indigenous to this area. The octopus here is single sucker and is tough, you don't get tender Mediterranean octopus. That's a bit frustrating. We haven't got any tuna either for the same reasons.

Things like cuttlefish are great when it's in season, but it's rarely cooked right (either over or undercooked) but Japanese chefs know how to use it.

If you could have one meal anywhere… where would you have it?
There's a restaurant I haven't been to but I really want to try, Asador Etxebarri, a grill restaurant in San Sebastian. I've been to San Sebastian twice, the first time I visited all the 3* restaurants and on the second trip I discovered the little tapas and pintxos bars. The fine dining restaurants don't capture where you are, but the bars are outstanding. We spent four nights in a row doing tapas bar crawls… everywhere you look you worry you've missed somewhere and you want to try more. There's one in particular (Ganbara), which is packed shoulder to shoulder, the diners spill out onto the street, eating spider crab tarts, plates of porcini with raw egg yolks, little prawns and anchovies, and great wine…

And finally… if you were on a desert island and only allowed three ingredients, what would you have?
I could catch my own fish and harvest my own salt… that's two of the most important things. I could probably make vinegar too. I think good oils are so important, more than butter, so that would be my first luxury. I'm obsessed with marmite so I'd definitely take that. I could try to cook it with fish and after a while I'm sure I'd come up with a recipe… and last thing, I think probably cheese, good cheese.

TOM KAY

—

FOUNDER, FINISTERRE

Tom Kay was brought up near the sea on the marshes in Norfolk. After studying Marine Biology at University, he spent a brief time working as a chartered surveyor in London, before launching Finisterre.

Tom has always been passionate about cold-water surfing and it was this passion that, in 2003, led him to launch the Finisterre brand, from a flat above a surf shop in St Agnes.

Finisterre has grown to become a widely known and well-respected brand with surfers and non-surfers alike. Its workshop-headquarters and flagship store are still in the same town that it was launched, and Finisterre also have stores in Falmouth, Hawksfield, Exeter, Bristol and London.

Tell us your story - what inspired you to start Finisterre?

Finisterre was really born from my love of the sea and of cold-water surfing. Back in 2003, this was the world that I knew, yet I struggled to find a product that was relevant to my lifestyle and to me - either in its function or how it was made - there was no sustainability agenda at all. So I started Finisterre to address these needs. Finisterre is built around three points of commitment – product, environment and people.

What does the name 'Finisterre' mean?

Finisterre means 'end of the land/earth' in French and used to be an area on the BBC shipping forecast. From an early age, this is a forecast I can remember listening to and learning to understand when I was in my parents' car. I used to imagine small boats miles out to sea in these huge storms, maybe with a crew sat around a radio set listening to the forecast, hoping for the wind and waves to abate, yet I was safe and warm in a car. It's an image that has really stuck with me.

And what brought you to Cornwall?

I'd been coming here on holiday since I was pretty young, so it's always been a place close to my heart.

How did the Finisterre brand grow in the beginning?

I started off by making a wind and waterproof fleece for cold-water surfers in my flat above a surf shop in St Agnes. The fleece was well made and because there was a story to the brand and a need for the product, we got good coverage. It was a great product that you still see around today!

How has the brand changed since the early days?

My vision of what the brand could become hasn't changed over the years and we still stand for what we did at the start. It has become more real in terms of the levels of innovation that we bring into our products and the fact that great people have joined the team and have helped steer the ship.

What do you feel has made Finisterre a success?

I think we have always been clear as to why

the brand exists and what we're here to do - to build the best and most sustainable products possible. We're also lucky to have so many great people that have come on board and push us forward.

Do you have a favourite product in your range, or one that you're most proud of?
The Bowmont programme is an unbelievable story: it's how, with the help of an Exmoor farmer, we helped resurrect a nearly extinct flock of British sheep and a 100% British supply chain to make some great knitwear and shirts. Our True North Range takes innovation and performance to a new level and the wetsuit development and recycling programme is something that I've been very close to.

We're aware that Finisterre is B Corps certified – can you tell us what this means and why it is important to you?
It's massive. Basically, B Corps certified businesses are the future of how businesses should be run. To become B Corps certified, we underwent a rigorous interview process covering all areas of the business and also altered our articles of association to reflect a legal commitment to people, environment, our products, and our communities in all that we do. For us this is something we've always done, so it's really an affirmation of the past 15 years, whilst giving us more to work towards and get better at in the future – that's a big part of it. I think we're the first European brand in our industry to become B Corps certified.

What other values are important to you for your business?
We have a few brand values that we live by – honesty, drive, passion.

You have some interesting collaborations with other companies and charities – can you tell us about some of these?
The RNLI collaboration was something that I really was proud of. I've been a crew member and helm on the St Agnes lifeboat for 15 years. It was great to work with such an iconic charity and raise some funds for them through the sale of the range.

It was also pretty big for us when VANS asked to collaborate on some styles, with the aim of bringing fabric expertise to the partnership and making some styles more weatherproof.

How have you seen Cornwall change in the time you've been here?
There's definitely more exciting business down here now. It's a really creative place to live and work, and there's a great business community.

Are there any up and coming brands in Cornwall that you're particularly excited about?
I meet lots of great start-ups when I do talks at universities and events. It's so good to see that this is happening in Cornwall. Surfers Against Sewage are really leading the charge on Plastic Free Coastlines.

When you're not in the Finisterre workshop, what do you like to do in your spare time?
Get in the sea with the family. My favourite places to go in Cornwall are Chapel Porth and Daymer Bay.

What advice would you give to someone thinking about starting up their own company or clothing brand?
There's no perfect time to start! If you wait for everything to be lined up, you'll miss the boat, so best to get going and work the rest out later.

What's next for you and for Finisterre?
The B Corps certification is big for us and for the future. We've got some really exciting products coming out as we continue to push innovation to achieve sustainability. There'll be a few more physical stores too.

FURTHER IDEAS

CAMEL VALLEY VINEYARD

One of Cornwall's oldest and largest wine producers, offering vineyard tours and tasting flights.

Nanstallon, Bodmin, PL30 5LG
01208 779 59
camelvalley.com

PRAWN ON THE LAWN

Boutique fishmonger and restaurant, with 24 seats and a menu that changes daily.

11 Duke Street, Padstow, PL28 8AB
01841 532 223
prawnonthelawn.com

PAUL AINSWORTH AT NO.6

Michelin-starred restaurant serving creative and playful dishes within an historic Georgian townhouse.

6 Middle Street, Padstow, PL28 8AP
01841 532 093
paul-ainsworth.co.uk

FINISTERRE

Cornish clothing brand making functional and sustainable garments for outdoor adventures.

Wheal Kitty Workshops, St Agnes, TR5 0RD
01872 554 820
finisterre.com

THE SORTING OFFICE

Quirky coffee shop in charming St Agnes, serving baked treats in a cosy setting.

Churchtown, St Agnes, TR5 0ZN
07807 324 088

PORTHMINSTER BEACH CAFÉ

Beachfront eatery with a menu of flavoursome dishes highlighting local produce and fresh seafood.

Porthminster Beach, St Ives, TR26 2EB
01736 795 352
porthminstercafe.co.uk

ST IVES BAKERY

Quaint neighbourhood bakery producing decadent sweet treats, rustic loaves and hand-crimped pasties.

Corner of Fore Street and The Digey, St Ives, TR26 1HR
01736 798 888

THE KITCHEN

Independent restaurant championing local produce and suppliers with a menu of small sharing plates.

Old Brewery Yard, High Street, Falmouth, TR11 2BY
07543 703 973

STONES BAKERY

Artisan bakery and café offering a wide range of freshly baked goods.

35 High Street, Falmouth, TR11 2AF
07791 003 183
stonesbakery.co.uk

THE HIDDEN HUT

Daytime café on the beach with a selection of simple dishes. Also hosts feast nights and events.

Porthcurnick Beach, Portscatho, Truro, TR2 5EW
hiddenhut.co.uk

WEEKEND JOURNALS

Editor: Milly Kenny-Ryder
thoroughlymodernmilly.com

Designer: Simon Lovell

Photographer: Gabriel Kenny-Ryder
gabrielkennyryder.com

All venues have been visited personally.

In loving memory of Granny Green who lived in Cornwall her whole life.

First Edition published in the United Kingdom in 2016.
Second Edition published in the United Kingdom in 2018.

Printed on FSC approved uncoated paper
ISBN: 978-1-9998591-1-4 (paperback)
ISBN: 978-1-9998591-2-1 (hardback)

hello@weekendjournals.co.uk
weekendjournals.co.uk